Making the Most of Your Time

Time-saving books that teach specific skills to busy people, focusing on what really matters; the things that make a difference – the *essentials*. Other books in the series include:

Making Great Presentations

Speaking in Public

Responding to Stress

Succeeding at Interviews

Solving Problems

Hiring People

Getting Started on the Internet

Writing Good Reports

Writing Great Copy

Feeling Good for No Good Reason

For full details please send for a free copy of the latest catalogue.
See back cover for address.

The things that really matter about

Making the Most of Your Time

Julie-Ann Amos

ESSENTIALS

Published in 1999 by
How To Books Ltd, 3 Newtec Place,
Magdalen Road, Oxford OX4 1RE, United Kingdom
Tel: (01865) 793806   Fax: (01865) 248780
email: info@howtobooks.co.uk
www.howtobooks.co.uk

British Library Cataloguing in Publication Data.
A catalogue record for this book is available from
the British Library.

Edited by Diana Brueton
Cover design by Shireen Nathoo Design
Cover copy by Sallyann Sheridan
Produced for How To Books by Deer Park Productions
Typeset by Anneset, Weston-super-Mare, Somerset
Printed and bound in the United Kingdom

NOTE: The material contained in this book is set out in good faith for
general guidance and no liability can be accepted for loss or expense
incurred as a result of relying in particular circumstances on
statements made in the book. Laws and regulations are complex and
liable to change, and readers should check the current position with
the relevant authorities before making personal arrangements.

ESSENTIALS *is an imprint of*
How To Books

Contents

Preface

Time management is a difficult skill to master. The balance between being a super-efficient, unapproachable machine and being efficient, effective and organised is a delicate one. No one wants to be so efficient they lose all enjoyment in what they're doing.

But the skills and techniques that make up good time management are very simple. A lot of them are common sense, and quick to implement. So why do so many people have poor time management? Simply, people fall into bad habits. They get used to doing things a certain way. It's not so much laziness as being *comfortable* with the way things are going.

Just a little effort to change a few things and you can have much more time at your disposal. This book contains practical advice on what to do, and how to do it. The aim is to make you more efficient and effective, which should make you feel happier at work.

Julie-Ann Amos

1 Understanding Time Management

You don't need more time in your day, you need to make more use of the time you have.

You can't increase or decrease, speed or slow time. We all get 24 hours in a day, no more, no less.

What you need to do is carefully manage your time, putting it to the best possible use. After all, it's one of the most important things we have at our disposal.

People often talk of **investing** money, but **spending** time. **Time is money** is a common phrase – and just notice how most of the words commonly used about time are money-orientated: we talk of buying, losing, making, saving, spending and wasting time.

Time management means **investing** a little time, making an effort to plan, organise, review, rearrange, sort and think. It can reap huge rewards.

The principles of time management are simple: **spend your time on actually doing things, not being busy**. Anyone can be busy, but you need to be busy on the **right things**.

IS THIS YOU?

● I can't start saying I'm too busy – people will think I can't cope with my job or I'm being uncooperative. ● I'm not a superhero! I can't do it all. ● If other people prioritised and didn't leave everything to the last minute, I wouldn't get so overloaded without warning. ● I don't like to compromise the standard of my work. Surely it's better to do a good job than rush work that isn't properly finished? ● But I like it all to be perfect. I just don't get the time to do my best work.

① SETTING LIMITS

In order to have enough time and manage it well, you need to set limits, because no one can fulfil all the demands made on them plus live their own life to the full. Setting limits isn't about saying no. It's about being realistic about what you can and can't do. Without any limits, we would all end up overstretched.

1. **Limit your availability**. Don't stop everything whenever the phone rings or someone walks in the door. These interruptions aren't necessarily more important or urgent than what you were doing. **Don't react, respond**. Think about what you're being asked and do what is best for all concerned. You don't have to have a reason for not reacting immediately – just say 'Can I get back to you, I'm in the middle of something important/urgent?' Limiting availability prevents you constantly stopping to deal with interruptions.

2. **Limit the time spent on a task**. Some things take a great deal of time for very little result. Pareto's Rule (or the 80/20 rule) says we spend approximately 80% of our time

doing work that produces only 20% of the result. Unless jobs are important, there is little point in this. Set sensible limits on how long you will spend on something, and if it takes longer, evaluate whether you really need to finish it, considering what else you have to do. You may have to sacrifice a feeling of accomplishment from completing things to save time!

3. **Limit priorities**. Everything isn't important, and everything can't have equal priority. Check how important something is when you receive work – don't just assume. You can't do everything, so remember Pareto's Rule – spend most of your time on the most important work, and if you have to skimp on time, skimp on things that *aren't* important.

80% of effort	20% of results
20% of effort	80% Of results

The 80/20 rule.

4. **Limit your involvement**. With good intentions, people often become overcommitted. We need to limit our involvement in things, so we work only on what we *should* be using our time on. Most of us like being involved – it's nice to have a finger in lots of pies, to feel necessary and needed, even important. But it can also take up too much time.

5. **Limit quality standards**. For most things we do, there is an acceptable standard, and if there isn't we mentally set one. Are you setting sensible standards? Artificially high standards take a lot of time to achieve, often for little or no reward except a sense of personal satisfaction. **Do things well enough**. Doing them better than necessary is a waste of time.

6. **Limit your sense of urgency**. It may sound crazy, but not rushing into things can often save time! Not everything needs doing today, but often we over-emphasise a task's urgency, like its importance. We feel we must do things *now*, and that they can't wait – think of it as hurry-sickness. It only leaves you rushed to deal with the really urgent matters.

What's the best use of my time right now, and why aren't I doing it?

 SETTING GOALS

Setting goals has a number of advantages. Goals can:

- increase motivation
- raise self-confidence (when you achieve them)
- help you achieve more
- help you decide how to spend your time

- improve performance

- increase personal satisfaction when you achieve them

- improve concentration

- help you suffer less from stress and/or anxiety.

When you set goals, **set positive goals** phrased in a positive way:

eg: deal with Jane more effectively, or be more assertive

not: don't give in to Jane so often.

Set specific goals – be precise. Give dates, times, amounts, numbers, rather than woolly goals. If you don't, you can't tell progress and check achievement.

eg: reduce cigarette smoking to eight per day

not: cut down smoking.

Set realistic goals. Base goals on what you want to achieve, not other people's expectations. Don't base goals on your ideal, your best performance, set them based realistically on what you can achieve without being over-optimistic. Goals you never achieve can demotivate.

eg: exercise at least one hour a week until June, then two
        hours per week

not: exercise a minimum of two hours per week.

Don't make your goals too easy – **stretch yourself**! If your goals don't stretch you, there's no point in having them!

Set goals for your **performance**, not for a set outcome. If you set goals based on outcomes, you lose control of your ability to achieve them. For example, setting a goal such as winning a race is dependent on the outcome of the race, which is dependent on *other runners'* performances, as well as your own. Instead, set goals based on *your own* performance, such as 'run the race in a personal best time'.

eg: increase my weekly exercise by 2 hours

not: exercise as much as Rob.

Keep goals **manageable**. For example, to buy a new car may be so large a goal you don't know where to begin! Break large goals down into small ones so that you can achieve them and see what you have to do next.

eg: 1. Pay off existing car loan. 2. Save £500 deposit. 3. Get car repaired to improve its selling price. 4. Buy new car.

not: buy a new car.

Once you've decided on your goals, **write them down**. Seeing things ticked off as you achieve them gives you a sense of accomplishment, and motivates you to do more.

Give **priorities**. Decide what to do first and number your goals accordingly. This enables you to focus your time and attention appropriately.

Finally, don't neglect setting **personal goals**. We can all too easily end up not achieving what we want with our lives. Take time to write down your personal goals. Consider all the things you want to do with your life. List them as goals. This will give you a means of prioritising and achievement *outside* of work, as well as in your job.

You'll never get what you want unless you sit down and define exactly what that is – and make a plan of how to achieve it. The most successful people make lists of goals, and go out to try to achieve them.

 GETTING ROUND THE BARRIERS TO TIME MANAGEMENT

Barrier 1 – control. The biggest mental barrier to time management is believing that other people and circumstances control our time. This is partly true, but there is a lot which you can do **to keep control of your own time**. Try not to be manipulated by people and/or events. If other people have open access to your diary, you lose control of what *you* want to do, and end up doing what others want you to do. Don't allow others unrestricted access to your diary – unless you trust them.

On the other hand, controlling your schedule and time *too* rigidly can mean that you aren't flexible. You won't be available to deal with emergencies. Keep some time free for emergencies, and you keep control of your time.

Barrier 2 – procrastination. Delays and postponements are part of life, but procrastination is *deliberately* putting off things which you ought to be doing. A little procrastination isn't too bad – but it stores up trouble. Things won't disappear just because you ignore them.

Eventually, you will end up with too much to do in one day, and so something will be missed. And starting every day with a large number of left-over tasks is daunting. **Do things now**.

Barrier 3 – immediacy. The opposite of procrastination is *immediacy* – wanting to do everything now – not being able to bear the thought of leaving things to wait. Think of it as 'hurry sickness'. It's often the reason why so many people work long hours.

Immediacy is often self-defeating. Working longer and longer to finish more and more means we get tired, then we make more mistakes, and we work slower. So like a hamster on a wheel going nowhere, we carry on working away, achieving less and less, to a lower and lower standard.

Barrier 4 – optimism. Positive thinking is a good thing. But being too optimistic is being unrealistic. Optimists are good starters of work, but poor finishers.

- Be realistic.

- Don't let rosy thoughts take over common sense.

- Don't take on more than you can achieve.

- If you aren't sure, say so, don't just commit to something.

- Keep some time back for emergencies.

- Finish what you start.

- Schedule finish times, or *deadlines* for tasks, not just start times.

   Barrier 4 – perfectionism. Perfectionists set impossibly high standards, and then set about trying to achieve them. The problem is that enough is never enough. There is always more information to be obtained, more ideas to think of, more people to consult or to discuss with, and so on. Perfectionists are also good starters, but poor finishers.

- Do things well enough.

- Don't focus on quality at the expense of quantity.

- Don't miss deadlines to do work to a better standard.

- Don't set standards above those of the people you are carrying out the task for – unless you really can afford the time.

- Schedule deadlines or finish times for tasks, to make sure you don't lose sight of the end of the task in the detail.

Don't let things stand in the way of managing your time well. You need to focus on what you want to achieve, and be willing to go to a little extra effort to achieve it. Then you can start saving time for the things you want to do.

REAPING THE REWARDS

Good time management can be hugely beneficial. The time you save will give you more time to do what you want. But you can also gain a number of other benefits:

- improve availability
- improve decision-making
- improve health
- improve productivity, efficiency, effectiveness
- make you easier to live with
- make you easier to work with
- make you feel more relaxed
- minimise the risks you take
- reduce stress.

Being busy may look good, but it doesn't always achieve very much. It would be better to be achieving lots, but looking less busy – and it would feel a lot less stressful, too.

MAKING WHAT MATTERS WORK FOR YOU

✓ Invest time now to save time later.

✓ Don't react, respond. Set appropriate limits so that you can achieve more.

✓ If you don't know where you're going, you'll never get there. Setting goals will keep you on track to achieving what you want to achieve.

✓ Understand what stands in the way of you managing your time well, and invest now in getting round the obstacles.

✓ Remember the benefits good time management can bring – it's worth a little effort to try to improve time management skills.

2 Contrasting Effectiveness and Efficiency

Do the right things (effectiveness) in the right way (efficiency) to get the most out of your available time.

Managing your time well depends on two things – **effectiveness** and **efficiency**. Both are important, but few people understand the difference between the two.

Effectiveness means being productive, being capable of achieving. It's about **doing the right things**. Effectiveness is about choosing **what** to do – and what not to do.

Efficiency means working effectively with the least waste of effort. It's about **doing things the right way**. Efficiency is about choosing **how** to do things.

Good time management is about spending the maximum amount of time **doing the right things well**. It's about both high effectiveness and high efficiency – finding out what you should be doing, and then doing it in a way that gives best results. Focusing effort on this will make you more productive.

Knowing what needs doing, and how best to do it is, after all, a pretty reasonable definition of someone who's good at their job!

IS THIS YOU?

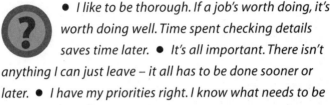

- *I like to be thorough. If a job's worth doing, it's worth doing well. Time spent checking details saves time later.* - *It's all important. There isn't anything I can just leave – it all has to be done sooner or later.* - *I have my priorities right. I know what needs to be done, I just can't see how to do it all in the time I have available.* - *I just can't seem to do anything right! If I rush I make mistakes. If I take my time, I can't meet the deadline.* - *What's the point! There's so much to do I can't ever get it all done anyway.*

 BEING EFFECTIVE

Effectiveness is about **doing the right things** – deciding what to do, and just as importantly, what not to. Be ruthless – no one can do everything, so you really do need to **be selective**. The less time you spend doing things you shouldn't, or don't need to, the more time you have for things you **need** to do.

Make a time log. This is one of the most effective means of measuring your effectiveness. Spend one working week noting down how long you spend doing everything – and I mean everything! All you have to do is to write down every time you do something, what you are doing and the time you start doing it. This will enable you to work out how much time you spent on each thing, then you can group activities and categorise them. The following list contains some common categories:

- meetings

- discussions

- waiting for meetings/appointments

- travelling
- writing – papers, proposals, notes
- telephone – taking and making calls
- dealing with interruptions
- answering queries
- handling email
- answering correspondence
- don't forget all those cups of coffee, trips to the loo, chatting to colleagues, sitting and thinking.

When you have the results, add up the time spent on the various activities. Then take a long, hard look at where your time went. Ask yourself some questions:

- Are you surprised about where your time went?
- What things did you spend a lot longer on than you realised?
- Did you really spend your time wisely?
- How many things did you do that weren't a good use of your time?
- More to the point, how much time did you use doing them?
- How much time could you save by cutting out some of the non-essential or unimportant things?

Of course I know what needs to be done. There's just so much other stuff that gets in the way . . . I sometimes don't know where it all comes from.

WORKING EFFICIENTLY

Efficiency means functioning effectively with minimum wasted effort. It's about **doing things in the right way, or the best way possible.** To be efficient, you need to take a long hard look at **how** you do what you do. Improvements are often possible, when you look afresh at the situation.

1. Could you do things more easily? Make a list of what would help you achieve this.

2. Are there tasks you could do faster? Add to the list anything that would help. Typical ideas might include fax machine, mobile phone, an answerphone, or a training course to improve your skills.

3. Can processes be improved? Now add to your list of ideas the people you would need to speak to in order to change processes to make your own job easier.

Time spent on these questions will reap rewards in efficiency later. You now have a list of things that you can use to improve your time management.

Consider training and development also. This doesn't just mean training courses, it means reading, talking to people, learning from others, finding out information. All this can help you save time and use the time you have wisely. Here are some examples:

- Areas such as typing, using technology, meetings, etc often involve skills people have had little or no training in. Ask yourself whether training or just an update would help you. For an example, a one-day course in handling meetings may make your meetings more efficient and shorter. That one-day course could save you 20 minutes each time you hold a meeting in future – saving you whole days each year! Then remember, everyone at the meeting saves that amount of time too – that one-day course really could be a good time investment.

- Often new techniques can save people a great deal of time. Try to keep abreast of new developments – not just training courses and seminars, but reading magazines and articles.

- See how others do things, and learn from them where possible. Talk to people. Ask around – has anyone got any bright ideas for streamlining things, or doing things differently? You can't think of everything, so don't try. Get help.

You don't have to make big changes. Changing 25 things by 1% adds up to a 25% change. Small changes all add up and can buy you valuable time.

 UNDERSTANDING IMPORTANCE AND URGENCY

Importance and urgency are used to identify high and low priority work. What you really need to establish is: **What's the best use of my time right now?** Faced with a workload, what should you do first? Ask yourself two questions:

- Is this task essential to my job, objectives or organisation?

- Is this task necessary but not absolutely essential?

If the answer to both is no – don't do it! Delegate the task, give it back, or discard it. It's not giving you any benefit. It's not even necessary.

We often confuse importance and urgency. If you were asked to decide what to do first, most people would choose something important. But if you think about it, **just because something's important, is it urgent?**

Does it have to be done *first*? Of course not.

Important things are important – which doesn't mean you have to drop everything and do them right away, but it means you have to do them, and do them properly. For example, birthdays are important. But you don't rush out on the first of January and buy all your birthday cards and presents and send them off! You wait until the right time (you could call it the *deadline*), and *then* you send them. Birthdays are important, but they're not always urgent.

If you don't remember a birthday until the day before, however, that's a situation where it becomes *urgent*, rather than important. See the difference? Importance and urgency really aren't the same thing at all.

There's so much to do – I don't know where to start, really . . . It's all got to be done. I need to set some time aside to look at it all and make some decisions, rather than just getting stuck in all the time.

 ASSESSING IMPORTANCE AND URGENCY

You can assign a simple priority system using the table below, with the letter A, B, C, or D for each task.

	IMPORTANT	NOT IMPORTANT
URGENT	• A tasks – both important and urgent. Do them now and do them well.	• B tasks – urgent, so do them quickly. But not important, so don't spend too long on them.
NOT URGENT	• C tasks – important but not urgent. These need to be given sufficient time to get them done properly. They deserve time and effort. Make sure you don't leave them too long, or they will creep up one box and could become urgent!	• D tasks – neither important nor urgent. Don't spend any time at all on these things until everything else has been done. Even then, take time to decide whether you should really be doing these things at all. If possible, negotiate with colleagues to drop these activities.

Importance Vs urgency

The trouble is, we get so caught up in things that we tend to treat everything as urgent. It's not being able to see the wood for the trees. We might actually be better off treating important things as if they were non-urgent, because then perhaps they would get the time and attention they deserve, instead of being rushed.

 MAKING 'TO DO' LISTS

Most people use lists in some way or another, if only for remembering shopping! 'To do' lists are very simple, but they are also very powerful and effective, because they have two effects:

● They get you organised, and make sure you don't forget what needs to be done.

● They can greatly reduce the amount of stress and worry that you have, by literally taking things off your mind and transferring them onto paper. When you are less stressed and have a clear head you can think better and do things more easily.

Some people don't bother. But using part of your brain to hold a list of tasks means that part isn't available for productive work. Plus it can weigh you down and prevent you being creative.

There are some basic guidelines for making lists.

1. **Get things off your mind**. Write them all down, without worrying about order, priority, etc – you can categorise things later.

2. **Break up large tasks** into smaller bites.

3. **Prioritise** the list, as shown in the table on page 23. Then simply deal with A tasks first, then B and so on. Within this, you can decide your own priorities. If there are three

A tasks to be done, for example, some people like to do the shortest first so they feel they are making progress. Others do the longest first so things get easier as the day goes on. The choice is yours, but as a rule of thumb, do tasks in the broad order A, B, C and D.

4. **Remember to re-prioritise** the list regularly, as priorities change over time – what wasn't urgent yesterday may well have become urgent today!

5. **Rewrite the list**. Cross off things once they are finished. This will feel satisfying, and clarify the priorities for you.

Making a list takes time, but it's time well spent. The relief from clearing your mind from juggling all the things it has to remember can be enormous.

MAKING WHAT MATTERS WORK FOR YOU

✓ Aim to be effective – doing the right things. Be ruthless with things that aren't important or worth your while doing.

✓ Be efficient. Invest time in looking at how to do things better – you will regain time spent in this way in the long run.

✓ Understand the difference between importance and urgency, and prioritise accordingly. Don't get side-tracked into dealing with low priority work at the expense of more important and urgent tasks.

✓ Don't get caught up in things – step back and always keep at the back of your mind 'How urgent is this? How important is it?'

✓ Make a 'to do' list and invest time in keeping it current. It will take a weight off your mind!

3 Planning

Planning is what will stop you from rushing off and doing things without making sure you're doing the right things, in the right way. Taking time to plan will save you huge amounts of time in the long run.

5
things that really matter

1 **KEEPING A DIARY**

2 **MAKING A SCHEDULE**

3 **AVOIDING OVERCOMMITMENT**

4 **USING YOUR SPARE TIME**

5 **STOPPING POWER GAMES**

Planning means taking your 'to do' list and diary, and planning what you will do when. Taking a small amount of time to plan before you start anything will make your work more effective and/or efficient. Most people think in vague terms: 'I'll do that later', 'that needs doing this week sometime', or 'I'll do that on Thursday afternoon'. But then things crowd in, and the time earmarked isn't available. This happens because the time hasn't been properly planned and reserved for the task.

Don't have too complex planning systems. These can take more time to plan than you spend working! Make plans flexible enough so that you can adapt to circumstances. Set goals or objectives, so you really know what needs doing.

Don't over-plan: not starting until every detail is planned, getting bogged down with the detail instead of getting on with the work.

IS THIS YOU?

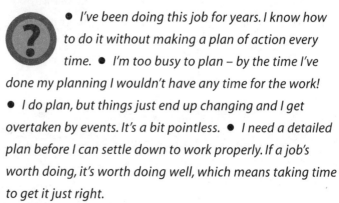

● *I've been doing this job for years. I know how to do it without making a plan of action every time.* ● *I'm too busy to plan – by the time I've done my planning I wouldn't have any time for the work!* ● *I do plan, but things just end up changing and I get overtaken by events. It's a bit pointless.* ● *I need a detailed plan before I can settle down to work properly. If a job's worth doing, it's worth doing well, which means taking time to get it just right.*

① KEEPING A DIARY

Diaries take care of the big things – birthdays, days off, holidays, training courses, meetings. You **make appointments** in your diary. When you have a meeting or appointment, schedule it in the diary, allowing adequate time for travelling both ways and don't underestimate how long the appointment will take. It is better to over-estimate the time, and then if the appointments takes less you have some unexpected extra time.

Batch activities. There are big advantages to doing small tasks in batches. Diarise time to do these on a regular basis, so they are taken care of. You can schedule in time to make telephone calls: for example, first thing in the morning and immediately after lunch. Then whenever you get a message to call someone, add it to your list of calls to be made and deal with it during the next telephone time. In a similar way, routine correspondence can be dealt with, say, twice a week, depending on how much of it there is.

Booking time in your diary isn't just for other people – book time for yourself to do things you need to get done.

MAKING A SCHEDULE

Block out any fixed time commitments, eg regular meetings, holidays, organised appointments. Remember to block out some time for living – allow time for eating lunch, coffee, toilet, etc!

Block in some time for **planning and scheduling – organising yourself** and your day. This needs to be at the beginning or end of each day.

Keep flexible. Always allow some time for unexpected events, interruptions etc. Ideally, allow two hours a day (or at least one if you really can't). After all, you can always fill the time with routine work if nothing happens, so don't be alarmed by the thought of blocking the time out.

Add in some time for batched tasks, as above – telephone calls and routine correspondence, plus any other tasks which are part of your job that you can do in batches. **Allow time for routine tasks**. Perhaps there are some regular updates, reports, or weekly checks for example. These can be scheduled in for each week on the appropriate time and day.

Every day, **check your schedule** for tomorrow. Is it realistic? Can you achieve it? If not, move things around; reschedule events where you can until it's workable. If you *are* going to have to move things around, don't leave it until the last minute, which can greatly inconvenience others. Do it the day before, so they can reschedule *their* time accordingly as well.

Try to plan in **variety**. For example, don't have a whole day of meetings! Lack of variety is caused by batching taken too far, and you will get tired of meeting after meeting, as well as having no time to write up notes or act on what was discussed. Try to batch small tasks, but where you have a lot of similar large tasks, spread them about if you can. Lack of variety will simply make you bored, and it's hard to do good work when you're bored.

A schedule is a detailed diary – for one day only. It tells you exactly what you need to do and when you have time to do it. It prevents distraction, overcommitment or missed deadlines. So why do so few people use them? It doesn't make sense.

 AVOIDING OVERCOMMITMENT

It's a shame there isn't an instant cure for overcommitment. Wouldn't it be lovely if whenever you opened your diary or schedule and you saw too much to cope with, you could just take two overcommitment tablets and it would all miraculously become manageable? Unfortunately, the only trick to handling overcommitment is to **avoid it** – not to let it happen in the first place.

Avoiding it *is* possible, it just isn't always easy. The following suggestions aren't magic, but if you try to use as many of them as you can, their combined effect should be sufficient to keep your diary and schedule from overflowing on a regular basis.

Be assertive:

- Don't be afraid to say no.

- If something isn't your job, say so.

- If you don't know how to do something, say so.

- If you don't want to do something, say so.

- If you haven't got time, say so.

Control your diary/schedule:

- Don't be afraid to reschedule to fit in things that are more urgent or important.
- Don't have too much empty space in a diary or schedule – schedule in tasks such as phone calls etc.
- Don't isolate yourself. If you don't leave a diary when you go out, people may take the risk of scheduling you for things without checking.
- Don't let others access your diary or schedule unless you trust them.

Query people:

- Always ask yourself if this is really a good use of your time. If not, ask whether you really need to do it.
- Always ask how urgent is this? How important is it? This helps you prioritise effectively.
- Ask *when* things need to be done, so you can set deadlines.
- Ask *who* else is working on something – maybe you can pool ideas and resources to get a job done in half the time.
- Ask *why* you need to do something if you are not sure whether you should do it or not.

Being overcommitted is unpleasant, and leaves you feeling rushed and hassled. Avoid overcommitment by taking preventive action.

 USING YOUR SPARE TIME

Have you ever considered how much time you have 'spare' – that is, time available but which you don't currently make use of?

- arriving early for meetings or appointments
- commuting
- driving
- on the bus, coach or train
- queuing
- time between appointments or meetings
- travelling
- waiting for others who are late
- waiting for transport.

And these are only a few of the potential sources of unproductive time!

For some, these unproductive times are welcome breaks in the working day. Trains are often full of commuters going to and from work with their heads in a book, gazing out of the window daydreaming, or even sleeping. For some, working on the move would increase stress levels.

But some busy people *would* benefit greatly from an extra hour in the day. And you can find it simply by utilising travelling and waiting time, converting them from unproductive into productive time.

You have two choices:

- try to avoid waiting time, and
- plan to use it.

Be prepared. Carry a little work around with you, so that you can use free time effectively. This doesn't mean armfuls of paper or heavy briefcases, just a folder of reading from your reading pile with you, to read in odd moments. This is one of the best ways to keep on top of reading. Also, take documents for checking – you can read and check these quickly and easily in a few spare minutes.

Decide how to travel. Consider *how* you travel, as well as *when*. For example, travelling by train rather than driving can be more relaxing, less stressful, more predictable and more productive because you can work on the train.

Equip yourself appropriately. If you have a laptop/portable computer, you can use that to good effect. Consider what other things would help you: a mobile phone, for example.

Arrive early. Optimise waiting time by planning to leave and arrive early – thus taking advantage of the time you will have to yourself before the meeting or appointment starts. Also, if you experience delays en-route, you will still be on time or just a little late, rather than being seriously delayed.

Know what needs doing. As a bare minimum, you should aim to carry your 'to do' list with you everywhere. That way you can use time to make calls, draft correspondence etc. If nothing else, you can use this usually unproductive time to rewrite your list regularly, a job which often gets overlooked because we can't make the time to do it!

Teach yourself something new while travelling. Consider listening to business books on cassette, or educational materials. Or read books on management, or other topics relevant to your work.

Confirm appointments and meetings before you leave for them. That way you will eliminate wasted journeys if there has been a mix-up, or if the meeting/appointment has been cancelled or is running late.

Don't be seen to be idle – don't *be seen* to arrive too early. When you arrive early, find somewhere else where you can work, use the telephone, or have a coffee and read. If you are seen to be waiting, people often assume you have plenty of time, and they tend to be less concerned about taking up your time or keeping you waiting in future.

You can find a lot of extra time by being smart about using odds and ends of time that would be otherwise 'lost', such as travelling or waiting for others.

 STOPPING POWER GAMES

Don't play power games. If people regularly keep you waiting, or behave inconsiderately, try to stop them. They may be playing power games with you. The only ways to prevent these games are to win them consistently (which is almost impossible without knowing the 'rules'), or to put an end to them. Here are some suggestions to try to put an end to these games.

- If a meeting or appointment is repeatedly late, ask politely if the other person or people could come to you, so that you can avoid being kept waiting.

- If a particular meeting always starts late, get there on time, and then leave a message saying what time you left and where you can be contacted, and leave the room until you are summoned because everyone is ready to start. This makes the point, politely.

- If you can afford to leave before a meeting or appointment starts, leave after 15 minutes or so. Say politely that you can't wait, and it will have to be rescheduled. This conditions people not to keep you waiting in future.

- Work while you are waiting, and when the person you have been waiting for arrives, ask if *they* wouldn't mind waiting for *you*, while you finish what you are doing.

*Spending your time making other people feel better is silly. Stop
people from playing power games with you, which only eats away at
your time.*

MAKING WHAT MATTERS WORK FOR YOU

✓ Keep a diary to keep track of the big commitments, things/dates to
remember, deadlines, appointments etc.

✓ Make a schedule to pin down exactly what you will do each day –
and what you won't! It's the key to keeping your workload
manageable.

✓ Avoid becoming overcommitted, because once this situation has
arisen it's too late to do much about it. Schedule carefully to make
sure you leave contingency time available to deal with the
unforeseen.

✓ Consider trying to make better use of your 'free time' such as
travelling time, time waiting for others, etc.

✓ Don't let people manipulate you into doing things to their own
schedule. Stop them playing games and eating into your time.

4 Delegating and Dealing with People

Delegating is giving part of your work to someone else to do – and making sure they are able to do it by giving them the necessary authority and responsibility.

We want to be *effective*. This means **using our time to do the right things.** Then we do those things *efficiently*, which means **doing them in the best way.** Prioritising and planning are about handling those things you *are* going to do. Interruptions take you away from the task at hand, and handling them well can save a lot of time. Handling people is a skill which is also used in delegation.

Delegation is giving someone the authority to carry out part of your job for you, or some task that is part of your job. It isn't about dumping a job onto someone else, nor is it about supervising someone doing something whilst you watch and criticise. It's giving someone the freedom and responsibility/authority to take something on for you. The whole idea is that it frees you up to do other things, whilst giving them something different to do. It's a very powerful way of maximising your available time.

IS THIS YOU?

 • *I can't delegate – people would take over. I'd look useless if others could do my work for me.*
• *I can't take the chance – no one else can do this quite the way it needs to be done.* • *It would take me so long to explain I might as well do it myself.* • *I'd love to delegate, but I don't have anyone to delegate to!* • *I have so much to do that by the time I stop to explain something, I'll have missed another deadline.*

① FEELING SAFE DELEGATING

Delegation is probably the single most important thing you can do to generate more time for yourself. It has several advantages for you and for the other person.

Advantages for you:

- Gives you more time.

- Gives you freedom to concentrate on and do other things.

- You're less vulnerable in emergencies: work can be maintained in your absence.

Advantages for others:

- They develop new skills.

- They can use their existing skills fully.

- They feel involved, and therefore more satisfied and happy in their work.

- Morale will be good.

- There will be fewer delays while people wait for you to make decisions – they will be able to decide themselves.

Delegation is one of the single biggest time savers you can use. Imagine a well-oiled machine, working away in your absence to get tasks done without you having to do anything but get it started and check the result.

 CHOOSING THE RIGHT TASKS AND PEOPLE

Don't delegate tough tasks beyond their skills or capabilities. Everyone likes a challenge occasionally, but if they fail or make mistakes it demotivates, and may make people wary of taking tasks from you again.

Don't delegate critical tasks – so crucial that failure would cause huge problems. It's not fair unless you are absolutely sure they can do the job, to the required standard and by the deadline. Otherwise this is an unfair burden.

Beware of delegating tasks that have been delegated to you. If someone has delegated something to you, maybe they feel *you* are the right person for the task. Check before delegating these tasks on to others.

Typical tasks for delegation usually fall into several categories:

- **Routine tasks** carried out at regular intervals can be easily delegated to someone with a steady workload, so they can plan in the additional work.

- **Easy tasks**, not requiring special skills, can be delegated to someone junior, to give them a little more responsibility and make them feel valued.

- **Time-consuming tasks** can be given to people with low workloads, or those who like work involving attention to detail.

- **Long-distance tasks** that are not pressing just yet can be easily delegated.

- **Tasks requiring specialist knowledge or skill** can obviously go to people who have that knowledge or skill – or you could train someone else so that more people have the necessary skills and knowledge.

When deciding whether or not to delegate to a particular person, ask yourself the following questions.

- Do they have the time to do the task?

- Do they have the ability?

- If not, can you train/coach them?

- Would they enjoy it?

No one likes to work with or for someone who gives them all the rotten jobs – and the definition of a rotten job is one you don't like doing. You can't overestimate the effect on morale if you give people work they like doing, and that expands their skills and knowledge, giving them responsibility on a regular basis. And if you don't know what they like doing, ask them!

 DELEGATING PROPERLY

Step 1 – communicate. Explain what the task is and why you are delegating it. Encourage them to take ownership of the job. *Always* tell others what you are delegating to whom. That way, people have your backing and the authority to get what they need.

Step 2 – agree the limits. You are responsible for the task being done correctly. You give the other person **accountability** – the ability to be held accountable for the job, the authority to do the job. You need to agree what support, help, advice etc you will provide to the person you are delegating to. Do they need any training? Resources? Additional help? It is no good someone coming to you and explaining that they cannot complete the task if you have then filled your time with other tasks, so you cannot assist. Agree what help they need to do the job beforehand, so you can plan accordingly.

Step 3 – set objectives. Be absolutely clear about the task, and communicate this to the other person.

- What standard is it to be carried out to?
- What progress checks will you be making?
- What is the deadline?

You can do this by setting objectives. An objective is an agreed specification for a piece of work. For example: 'To calculate by next Friday the budget spent so far this year under all categories, by cost centre, and to summarise this on one sheet.' As you can see, this is a quite detailed matter – far more complicated than just saying 'John, can you get me a budget analysis by next Friday?' Proper objectives are SMART:

S – specific

M – measurable

A – achievable

R – realistic

T – time-related (ie with a deadline).

Step 4 – let them get on with it. Having briefed people properly, let them get on with it; only now you have to make sure they carry on with the task without problems. It's quite a fine balance which isn't easy, letting people get on with a task and making sure they're all right.

Some people will be fine; others will feel they need ongoing support and advice. Whilst you should aim to give these when necessary, beware of people who never seem to be able to manage without them. Some people have a lack of confidence, which prompts them to keep checking that they are doing things correctly. They may need extra encouragement to try to stop this habit. Alternatively, try referring them to someone else so they don't get dependent on you. And don't forget to offer support even to those who don't seem to need it – some people are afraid to ask for help.

Step 5 – monitor progress. Monitoring is not checking. Monitoring means watching – seeing what is being done and asking people how they are getting on. It does not mean examining their part-finished work regularly to look for mistakes. If you are monitoring properly, you won't get too many mistakes – you will spot things and be able to intervene gently before they even arise. Try to just **be available**, not to lurk watchfully as if you are expecting things to go wrong. Just knowing that someone is there if they need them gives people confidence.

Step 6 – intervene promptly where necessary. If you do have to step in because you can see things are starting to go wrong, tread carefully. The last thing you should do is to take back the job – even though they may want you to! Talk things over and leave them to get on with it again, this time aware of where they were starting to go wrong. Delegation is highly dependent on people having the confidence to succeed – so never undermine people's confidence by threatening to take back the work, or worse, to get someone else to take it over. Even if they think they can't carry on with it, try to support them and let them try again.

This lets them know you trust them.

Step 7 – evaluate success. Once the delegated task is finished, try to have a review with the person who did it, even if it is only a few minutes. Check whether the objective has been met, and if not, why not. Find out how the other person found the task. They may need further training, or you may learn more about how to delegate in future. Of course, you could just look at the task and see whether it has been done well – without involving the other person. But feedback helps them to improve, and to know whether they have done well.

Delegation is a huge factor in success. People who delegate well not only save themselves time; they develop the skills and experience of those around them, which is highly motivational. Haphazard delegation doesn't help anyone. It risks the task and frustrates and demotivates people.

 MANAGING INTERRUPTIONS

Interruptions are incredible time-wasters. There are some effective techniques for managing them and making sure they don't eat too far into your time.

Technique 1 – drop hints to people

- Don't smile and look welcoming – you may risk seeming hard and potentially unfriendly, but you need people to understand you are busy.

- Look briefly at your watch or a clock, especially if someone says 'are you busy?' or 'have you got a minute?' *before* you say 'yes, what is it?' It can work wonders! It implies you really don't have long, so they really do need to be brief.

- Set an 'open door' time – a publicised time when you will

be available, so people can drop in. It discourages them from coming at other times, or if they do you can politely ask if it can wait for the 'open door' time.

- Stand up when someone is talking to you. It discourages them from sitting down, and implies that you are on your way somewhere and can't be delayed too long.

- Walk about – a management technique called MBWA – Managing By Wandering About. It means wander about and get out and see people, so if they need you, they can catch you then and there and you can deal with things at your convenience. If you walk about and are approachable regularly, people won't need to interrupt you apart from with real emergencies that can't wait. But be sensitive: MBWA is basically interrupting others, before they can interrupt *you*!

- When someone approaches you, don't stop what you are doing at once. Make them wait for a few seconds, thus giving them the hint that they are stopping you working. It's a good idea even to say 'hello' *before* looking at them, as it implies they are taking your attention away from what you were doing.

Technique 2 – making it hard for people to interrupt

- Close the door.
- Create visual barriers – something between you and the door. Plants, cupboards and screen are ideal.
- Don't sit facing an open door – it *invites* people to come and interrupt you!
- Have few (or no) free seats by your desk to discourage people. Also, they won't stay for long if they have to stand up.

- Put a 'do not disturb' notice on the door!

Technique 3 – plan for interruptions

- Allow time for interruptions – they are almost inevitable.

- Cooperate with colleagues. Get them to answer your calls for you so you can work uninterrupted, in return for a reciprocal arrangement when *they* need to work.

- Get out of your office and work somewhere where you won't be interrupted.

- Say 'no' – politely.

- Work earlier or later to avoid interruptions. See whether you can 'flex' your day to start and finish early or late. Early morning and late evening are times when there are few interruptions.

Interruptions are a part of life. It's hard to avoid them, as they wouldn't be interruptions if we knew when to expect them! It's best to allow some time for them, as they are so inevitable, and then learn some good techniques for limiting their invasion for when they do occur.

MAKING WHAT MATTERS WORK FOR YOU

✓   Delegation isn't anything to be afraid of. It has big advantages for both yourself and the person you delegate to.

✓   Delegate the right tasks, to the right people. It really is as simple as that.

✓   Delegate methodically, agreeing up-front what needs to be done, how, when, to what standard etc. Then monitor, don't check up on people, and finally assess how they have done and provide feedback.

✓   Be aware of what can go wrong and take steps to prevent it.

✓   Manage interruptions to minimise their occurrence, or to limit their duration when they do occur.

5 Dealing with Physical Organisation

Dealing with your surroundings and clearing your environment is a valuable tool in time management as it enables you to think clearly and to concentrate fully on the task in hand.

For many people, one of the most daunting things about getting organised is the paper mountain around them. This is often a molehill in disguise, when you actually go through it and analyse what you need to do with it. Just getting things rationalised into a system can bring intense relief.

Sorting things into piles for dealing with later is common practice. A common piece of advice used in time management to counteract this is to handle each piece of paper only once, or **do it now.** A better practice is to **handle each piece of paper twice**: once to sort it based on its priority, and then once to deal with it when its turn comes round.

Periodically **clear out backlogs** and **deal with long-standing tasks**. This will reduce stress as well – the real harm in backlogs is that they mentally and emotionally weigh you down, not that they take up too much space in your in-tray.

IS THIS YOU?

● I know I've a lot on my desk, but I like it that way. I need to keep my finger on the pulse, and have access to everything I need. ● I'd love to clear up, but quite frankly I just don't know where to start! ● It may not look like it, but I know just where everything is . . . ● I can never find anything around here. I had those papers only yesterday and now they've been moved. ● A tidy desk indicates someone who hasn't enough to keep them busy.

 ## CLEARING THAT DESK

Why do some people always have neat, tidy desks, whilst others have mountains of paper piled high, dotted with various bits and bobs? Well, it isn't because the fairies come in every night and mess up your desk, is it?

A cluttered, untidy desk usually doesn't indicate an excess of work: it indicates poor organisation. Too often, people use the amount of work which they have (especially paperwork), to excuse cluttered desks. But the more work you have, the more important it is to get your desk *organised*.

Your desk is for working on. Your desk is not:

- a coffee table
- a filing area
- a storage area
- something to sit on.

Untidy or cluttered desks are not good because:

- They increase error.
- They slow down progress/work.

- They increase distractions.

- It is harder to establish priorities.

- People judge with their eyes. Untidy desks tend to make people assume you have an untidy mind, poor self-discipline etc.

- It helps procrastination, by giving you lots of potential things to do to avoid doing the task in hand.

- You can't find what you want when you want it.

Clearing a desk is easy. *Keeping* it clear is the hard part! Here are some ideas which should help.

- Handle work as few times as possible.

- Have *one* tray only for incoming work. Do not let anyone put things on the desk: make them use the in-tray, so you don't lost control over where things are.

- Never *store* things on your desk.

- Throw things away! Be ruthless! Only keep what you *really* need.

- Try to allocate a small amount of time at regular intervals, say once a month, to clear your desk. Despite all our best intentions work builds up, and so does clutter. Programme in a tidy-up at regular intervals.

- Understand that volume of work is not the biggest problem: it's organisation.

You can't do efficient, effective work surrounded by clutter. It distracts and demoralises, and takes your focus off the main priority – the task in hand.

ORGANISING SHELVES AND SURROUNDINGS

Given that your desk is not a storage area, you do need to give some thought to shelves and storage areas.

Break your work area down into areas to make them easier to handle:

- bookshelves
- computer workstation
- cupboards
- desk
- drawers
- filing cabinet(s)
- shelves
- tables
- tops of filing cabinet(s).

Make life easy – keep things to hand. Decide which things you need to use or refer to most often, and have these things closest to hand.

Group items: batch or group items together for ease of use. Try to establish broad categories of things that can be grouped together. For example, here are some categories – but remember, this is not an exhaustive list – you have your own things:

- catalogues
- company information
- computer books/manuals
- files
- magazines and professional papers

- notes
- reading materials
- reference manuals
- reports
- stationery
- telephone directories.

Be ruthless!

- Anything you haven't used for two or three weeks can safely be stored.

- Banish personal photographs, knickknacks etc to a place where they won't get in the way or distract.

- Don't be afraid to put things away.

- Throw duplicates away.

- Little items such as stapler, hole punch, staple remover, tippex etc can be placed in a drawer – not out on your desk where they can be borrowed, get in the way and make you feel cluttered.

- Outdated information should be updated or discarded all together.

- Put all personal items – coffee stocks, toiletries, spare socks, umbrella etc in one place, preferably a drawer.

- Spend a few minutes at the end of every week (preferably every day) to tidy your workspace. By keeping on top of things in this way, they don't build up and take ages to sort out again.

Just ask yourself 'What's the worst thing that could happen if I threw this away?' If you can live with the answer, then throw it!

DEALING WITH CLUTTER

Clutter isn't just paper. It's all sorts of things: a coat over the back of a chair; papers spilling out of a waste bin; old coffee cups; dead flowers or plants; packaging from parcels or correspondence that has been opened; magazines; useful papers that you think you should hang on to in case they come in handy – the list is endless.

Clutter is disorder. But it's more than just a mess – it's a mess or disorder that interferes with other things. It gets in the way. Handling clutter isn't about being tidy, it's about being **free to do work without interference**.

Piles of paper is what most people think of when they think of clutter.

- Don't keep what you don't need.

- File loose papers. If there isn't a file, make one.

- File things whenever you can, to get them out of the way.

- File things where you can find them when you need them.

- Look realistically at things already filed and stored, and regularly assess whether you still need them.

Electronic clutter such as saved computer files and e-mails. The electronic office is great for some, but for others it just replaces the misery of an overflowing in-tray and desk with an overflowing mailbox and computer screen.

- File what you need to keep so it's out of sight but retrievable.

- Label things sensibly and meaningfully so they are easy to find.

- Don't send to more people than necessary when you send out your own e-mails – it only passes the clutter on.
- Don't be afraid to delete – it's quite painless (most of the time!).

Other stuff including coffee cups, coats, tissues, odds and ends. All the things you would tidy away if you were having important visitors, in fact.

Items waiting for other people to make decisions before these things can be actioned. Keep these to hand if the answer is expected imminently – today or tomorrow, say. If the response is likely to take longer, consider a file called 'awaiting response'. Then when you get the response, you can take the appropriate action and transfer the paperwork into the correct subject file.

Little pieces of paper – notes or sticky post-its. Throw them away if they've been dealt with. Don't be tempted to keep notes on scraps of paper just because they have useful details or contact numbers on – these should be transferred somewhere safer. Consider establishing a 'to do' system instead, and do away with all the notes.

Interesting things you don't know what to do with. File them. If you don't know how, set up a file called something like 'interesting bits and pieces', and keep them all in there!

Spring cleaning away all your clutter at regular intervals will save you a great deal of time in the long run. It's easier to be efficient when you appear efficient.

 CREATING A DAY FILE

A day file (sometimes called a 'tickler' file by Americans) is extremely useful, but something few people use. It's a file specially to remind you of future events, and to hold the papers for these events.

You often receive things that you will need in the future, but don't need yet. These need to be stored in a safe place, where you can find them when you need them quickly and easily. The obvious place is to have one file set aside solely for such items.

Creating a day file. Have a ring-bound folder with two sets of dividers in it. One set is numbered 1 to 31, and another is a set of 12, labelled for each month of the year. These types of file dividers can be easily purchased in most good stationers.

Suppose it is 1st January. You should put the 31 numbered file dividers at the front, followed by the 12 month dividers, starting with February and finishing with January.

Every time you need to store something for a future date, simply file it in the appropriate date 1–31 if it is required for January, and under the appropriate month if it is required *after* January. Every day, you just check to see what things are there for you.

At the end of the month, you simply remove all February's papers and file them by day appropriately, and place the February divider to the back of the file. This cycles the paperwork on a regular basis, so it doesn't get lost.

Examples of things that you would file in a day file:

- meeting agendas
- documents you have been asked to take to an appointment
- letters that need a reply by a certain date
- letters that need to be sent on a certain date

- lists of things to be done on that date
- maps and directions for getting to an appointment
- notes for a meeting or appointment
- social invitations.

A day file gets things off your desk, out of your in-tray and puts them in a place where they are easy to find. It helps you be prepared for events such as meetings and appointments and reduces the burden of having to remember where you put important things.

MAKING WHAT MATTERS WORK FOR YOU

✓ Clear your desk as much as possible – and keep it clear.

✓ Organise your surroundings so you know where everything *should* be – so that everything has a home.

✓ Get rid of as much clutter as possible. Having less things around you makes it easier for you to work.

✓ Create and use a day file. It will save you time and help you feel more organised and prepared.

6 Dealing with Paperwork and Administration

Dealing quickly and efficiently with administration leaves more time for your main task.

4

things that
really matter

1 FILING

2 DEALING WITH INCOMING MAIL

3 MANAGING YOUR READING

4 USING THE AVAILABLE TECHNOLOGY

Administration is part of every job – unless you are lucky enough to have a secretary or PA to organise and manage for you. Filing, incoming mail, reading, there are so many tasks to distract us from the one at hand. Dealing with these quickly and efficiently means minimum disruption to your main task.

People view administration as a menial task. It's actually quite important. Things like filing, checking and sorting incoming mail, etc can be really big influences on how you do your job. For example, incoming mail may contain facts or information which will alter how you do what you're currently working on.

IS THIS YOU?

● I hate filing! ● I can never find anything anyway, so what's the point of filing it? ● How can going through the post possibly be more important than actually working? ● I have a desk full of reading – not that I ever get time to read any of it . . .

FILING

Filing is something so simple that most of us do it without much thought. But people often have poor practices to do with filing, and these can cost us valuable time:

- Filing things by date rather than by subject – makes it hard to find things.

- Having lots of small files – makes it hard to find the right file.

- Having only a few huge files – makes it easy to find the right file, but hard to find things within it.

- Keeping files indefinitely – makes them too large.

- Never discarding or archiving old filing – creates pressure for space.

- Not keeping filing up-to-date – makes it impossible to find recent things.

- Not labelling files with a meaningful name or reference – means others cannot find anything when you're not around.

- Not remembering where you filed something – means your filing system needs re-designing.

There are several **methods of filing**: use the most appropriate one for the material you want to file:

- by subject
- by alphabetical reference, usually names or places
- by number
- by area
- by date.

Filing tips:

1. **Name all files.** Give files or folders a meaningful name, so that when you see the name you logically think of things that would go in that particular file. Use the first association your mind makes when you think of the things in the file. This means that when you are looking for something, your thought process should usually be the same, and you will be most likely to deduce in which file the document will be.

2. **Colour-code files and labels** where possible, to make it easy to see at a glance which file you need.

3. **Don't file** things that you can easily get from someone else when needed. This is a common bad filing habit, and only leads to enlarging your filing system unnecessarily.

4. **File odds and ends** (magazine articles, interesting snippets etc) according to the information they contain, not where you found them. For example, file articles and papers about management under 'management', rather than by the magazine or training course they came from.

5. File things within folders or files with **the most recent thing on top.** This will make it easier to find. Filing like this, in date order, should be used wherever possible.

6. **Set up a regular time** to go through files and get rid of old and unwanted material, so files stay manageable.

7. **Store files alphabetically.** If there are one or two files

which you use very frequently, maybe it would be better to keep these in an easily accessible place. Similarly, if a few files are used regularly by others, it might be wise to put these somewhere prominent, where they can be easily found without rummaging through your other files.

When unsure whether you need to file something or not, put it in a drawer, box or tray for a month. If you haven't needed to refer to it in that time, it's usually safe to file it.

 DEALING WITH INCOMING MAIL

Mail can't be controlled: you can't stop it when you're busy. So you need **efficient systems for handling it**. Every day sort through incoming mail and/or paperwork. This will mean looking through your in-tray at least once a day.

Don't be tempted to think that other things are more important than 'going through the post' – this is a very common mistake. After all, how do you know that something more important/urgent than your most important/urgent work hasn't just arrived? Or you could be wasting time doing something, while instructions to do it differently (or not to do it at all) are sitting in your in-tray.

Problems with in-trays:

- an in-tray used to hold reminders
- an in-tray becoming a filing system
- an in-tray which never reduces
- an over-flowing one
- not having one
- only going through it once a week
- sorting your in-tray and putting things back in it at the bottom

- the whole of your desk being an in-tray.

   Sorting mail in: when you go through your tray, everything you pick up must either:

- be dealt with then and there
- go into the 'today' pile, or
- go into the 'later' pile.

Here are some examples:

1. **Dealing with things immediately** doesn't mean filing documents or reading them immediately – it simply means getting them out of the in-tray and preferably off your desk.

- filing gets done (at least) weekly
- items for future dates go into the day file
- items for passing on get passed on
- items for reading go straight into your reading store
- unwanted items are discarded.

2. **The 'today' pile** contains correspondence, messages, papers that must be actioned today, plus papers that come out of the day file today.

3. **The 'later' pile** contains:

- correspondence that you need to think about
- non-urgent work
- papers to go into the day file for other days (see page 52)
- things you aren't sure what to do with
- what's left after you have removed the 'do now' and 'today' things!

Sorting tasks and mail in gives you one huge advantage. It lets you plan your day. When you have sorted, you know what the day holds in store for you (apart from the unforeseen emergencies and interruptions).

The point of going through the mail in is to reduce it. Anything that can be passed on, filed, discarded, or sent back should be done straight away. By hanging on to these things and dealing with them later, you are delaying the action they need and handling them more than necessary.

  MANAGING YOUR READING

Don't read things when you get them. Unless something is high enough priority that you need to read it straight away in order to take action, leave it for reading. Then allocate a little time each day or even each week for reading. **Sort your reading** – never just dig into the reading pile and start from the top down.

1. **Items to be retained but not actually read.** You don't actually have to read your reading – there is an enormous quantity of stuff you may need to keep for reference. These items should be filed, unread, by subject – so you can refer to them when needed.

2. **Items to be read.** Put these to one side, ready. You can take some of this with you when you go to meetings or travelling, to use any spare time profitably.

3. **Material to be passed on.** Material is often of more use to someone else than to you, so pass it on.

4. **Material for discarding.** Some material may turn out to be not worth reading after all, or out of date by the time you get round to sorting your reading. It can be discarded.

Prune your reading. If you need to read an article in a magazine, or a part of a paper, just keep the part you need. That way, you won't feel intimidated by the size of your reading pile. Generally speaking, cutting articles out is quicker than photocopying them, but if you want to file them photocopies can be neater.

Read actively:

- annotate
- highlight
- make notes
- underline.

All too often we think of reading as a passive process, where we sit and let the words enter our eyes and trickle through to the brain! You can help yourself read by helping the brain latch on to important facts, words and phrases. Making reading an active process means the brain doesn't switch off so easily, so you are less likely to suffer lack of concentration.

Consider photocopying a document if you need to, so you can do the above, if the document isn't yours to write on. Especially useful is photocopying things at a slightly reduced size. This gives you a larger margin for making notes (although beware of making them too hard to read!).

Read in as much depth as you need – if you only need a feel of the subject, skim through quickly, noting anything that jumps out at you. If you need to read a document properly, wait until you can give it your full attention.

Magazines and newspapers break a subject down into bite-sized amounts to be read. Reading one article on a subject takes far less time than reading a whole report or book. Also they tend to look attractive – especially magazine articles, which often include pictures, charts and diagrams to stimulate your interest.

One of the disadvantages of articles, however, is that they may not give you all the information you want. They also often take a useful topic, and pad it out with a lot of other text that you don't need – typically to make it look more attractive and interesting.

Try to set aside reading time every week (or twice a week if you have a lot of reading to do at work), of say half an hour – longer if you can manage it. This will ensure reading doesn't accumulate to the point that you lose the ability to catch up.

 USING THE AVAILABLE TECHNOLOGY

Today there is a huge range of technology and systems to assist us at work, but how many of us really appreciate what is available and how to make best use of it? Here are some tips to save time with technology.

- Use **conference calls or teleconferencing** to avoid attending a meeting, saving travelling time, or where you have to say the same thing to several people, delivering your message to them all at once.

- Use **electronic mail (e-mail)** instead of a fax where a document may have to be re-typed, so it can be electronically saved, edited and used to prepare other documents, saving large amounts of typing time.

- **Avoid printing and filing** by electronically filing e-mails like other documents. Do not print them unless *absolutely* necessary.

- Use e-mails to **avoid making telephone calls**, saving you getting caught up in conversations.

- Set up **autodial numbers** for the numbers you fax most frequently, and **polling lists** for groups of people to whom you want to fax the same document.

At work, your computer may be what is called a **standalone machine** – not connected to anything, or it can be **networked**. If your computer is networked, you can access things that other people can access and vice versa. This is called **common or shared access**. This can be invaluable in time management. Instead of sending people documents by post, fax or e-mail, just tell them where they are stored and they can read them for themselves.

Nowadays, an increasing number of telephones are **speakerphones**, or have a **hands free facility**. Use them to let others in the room listen, to save you passing on messages. Use one so your hands are free to take notes, even to type up the conversation as you speak, saving you writing things up later; or to listen to voicemail/answerphone messages, leaving your hands free to make notes.

Voicemail is a modern variant of the humble answering machine. There are a number of variants, but basically a telephone is programmed to take messages exactly like an answering machine. Use voicemail to buy yourself time – switch it on and get on with work free from interruptions. Or use it to record reminder messages to yourself, while you are away from your workplace.

Technology is there to help us, and much of it saves time – if you know how to use it. If you don't, it can waste a lot of your time instead.

MAKING WHAT MATTERS WORK FOR YOU

✓ Keep filing logical and up to date. It will make your life easier in the long run.

✓ Deal with incoming mail regularly, and before returning to tasks you were working on, sort it and deal with it as appropriate. This will prevent build-up.

✓ Manage your reading so it gets done where necessary and is available to read/use later if needed.

✓ Use available technology effectively to save you time and help you work effectively.